AVA
R

Translation
Blyth Wright

To Frédérique

Acknowledgements

I wish to thank Bruno Bagnoud, founder of Air Glaciers and of the FXB (Francois-Xavier Bagnoud) rescue organisation, whose support has been enormously encouraging.

I also thank all those who have made their contribution to this publication, by their personal accounts, their writings, their photographs or their suggestions: Francois Sivardière, director of ANENA (National Association for the Study of Snow and Avalanches), Pascal Fournier, Dominique Michellod, Nicolas Gaspoz, Pascal Gaspoz, Gerald Maret, the guides of the FXB rescue organisation, Jacky Michelet, director of OCVS (Valaisanne Cantonal Rescue Organisation), Michel Weber, Stephane Oggier, Urs Wiget, Gilbert Maury, doctors belonging to GRIMM (Mountain Rescue Doctors Group), Marc Schnider, helicopter pilot, and Martin Roduit, winchman at Air Glaciers, Jean-Francois Meffre, head of avalanche safety in Andorra, Jacques Mariethoz, ski coach, Marie-Jo Besson, Vincent Chritin, director of IAV Engineering, Robert Volponi, Didier Turc, ski patroller at L'Alpe-d'Huez, Bertrand Favre, head of safety at Ovronnaz, Francois Bloch, head of safety at Luz-Ardiden, and Jean Troillet, mountain guide.

Robert Bolognesi

Preface

Annapurna, West Face, 1985. There had been a huge amount of new snow. After two weeks of bad conditions, the good weather had returned. My companion Pierre-Alain Steiner and I began to climb. But the higher we climbed, the more knots I had in my stomach. It didn't feel right. I talked about it with Pierre-Alain and then we decided to turn back, giving up our dream for that year. It was the second time we had turned back, as we had done in 1984. When we had taken the decision, I immediately felt better. Even at the ends of the earth and after all the long preparations, one must have the strength to say 'No'.

Jean Troillet*

* *Jean Troillet, mountain guide, has climbed K2 (8611m), Dhaulagiri (8167m, first winter ascent), Everest (8848m), Cho Oyu (8202m), Shisha Pangma (8046m), Makalu (8481m), Lhotse (8516m) and Kangchenjunga (8516m). He has climbed many new routes on the highest mountains in the world and holds the world altitude record for a snowboard descent: 8700m on Everest.*

The first-known mountain rescue operations took place amongst the great alpine passes. The hospices, notably those of Little and Great St Bernard, played a major role; numerous travellers were saved by the monks and their dogs. In the 18th century the Alps were essentially the preserve of scientists. It was their insatiable curiosity which led to the exploration of the mountains, which in turn led to the development of the sport of alpine climbing. Subsequently this activity evolved in many directions, with winter ascents, guide-less ascents, aid-climbing direct ascents, then, more recently, with free-climbing and the amazing development of snowsport in all its expressions: touring, free-riding, extreme descents. In order to reduce the risks inherent in these activities, Robert Bolognesi gives us the benefit of his advice. He outlines a number of simple approaches and puts forward a learning process based on practical experience. After reading his book, perhaps we should consult our conscience, take a fresh look and set off again on a wiser path.

Pascal Fournier*

* *Pascal Fournier, mountain guide and helicopter pilot, is head of the FXB rescue organisation (Valais). His work has included several hundred mountain-rescue operations.*

Introduction

People say avalanches are unpredictable. Is that true? And even if it is, is that an excuse for throwing your life away?

It is certainly true that no-one is in a position to claim that they can predict every avalanche, and it has to be said that some are particularly baffling, even for the most experienced. Nevertheless, an avalanche is not a supernatural event, and one does not need to be able to describe the release mechanisms in all their complexity in order to identify the majority of hazardous situations. It is enough to be able to 'read' the mountain to reduce considerably the threat posed by the 'white death'.

This little guide will assist those who wish to undertake this apprenticeship. In the first instance it will give readers a wider understanding of the phenomenon, using not only objective data but also the accounts of witnesses and survivors. It will go on to reveal some of the indications which, for those who know how to interpret them, will enable a local assessment of avalanche hazard to be made and a number of pitfalls to be avoided. Finally, it will put forward some rules of thumb, be it for free-riders*, ski tourers, walkers or climbers, that will permit safer travel on the mountains.

*Experts in snowsport on all terrain, all snow types

Avalanches

Avalanches are not unusual events; ski patrols in large ski areas make controlled releases of several hundred avalanches each winter. But avalanches remain a source of mystery. However, it is essential to understand the phenomenon in order to assess the risk which it presents. Avalanches are described in this chapter by type (classification) and through personal accounts.

CLASSIFICATION

Before an avalanche occurs, snow forms in the atmosphere by the freezing of the water vapour in moist air containing condensation nuclei (dust, salt particles, etc). Depending on the particular atmospheric conditions, the snow crystals formed may be star-shaped (dendritic) or spherical (hail, graupel). Once on the ground these crystals, often combined into snowflakes, constantly undergo mechanical processes and energy fluxes which cause them to change (metamorphose).

Equilibrium forms are most common when temperatures within the snowpack are fairly uniform. The process starts with the breaking up of the star-shaped crystals and is fuelled by the transfer of material from the convexities towards the concave zones of the crystals, which is caused by instabilities in surface tension. The crystals round out, they reduce and become similar in size, while their numerous points of contact lead to the formation of ice bridges which weld them to each other (sintering). This phase of metamorphism also makes the snowfall densify and stabilises it.

Kinetic growth (formerly called 'temperature gradient metamorphism') occurs if the temperature variation at different levels in the snowpack is moderate or large (more than 5°C/metre). Gradients of these values are seen when the surface of the snowpack is subject to strong cooling and when the snowpack is shallow and of low density. Then the transfer of material takes place from the bottom upwards and forms faceted crystals ('squares'), then cup crystals ('depth hoar'), creating poorly bonded layers within the snowpack.

Melt-freeze metamorphism occurs when water (from rain or melting) is present within the snowpack. It leads to the formation of groups of large rounded crystals, either weakly bonded by capillary cohesion or, on the other hand, well bonded due to re-freezing. This is the only evolution possible for surface hoar, graupel and cup crystals. These changes occur more rapidly near the surface of the snowpack where the energy fluxes are stronger.

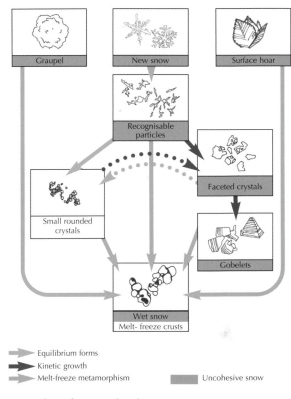

Metamorphism of snow (outline diagram)

In this way the sequence of weather events determines the layering and structure of the snowpack, its overall cohesion and, ultimately, its stability. The nature of the bonds between snow crystals (settling, sintering or capillarity), depending on their state of metamorphism, also determines the type of avalanche which is released. So we can distinguish:

• powder-snow avalanches (cohesion due to settling);
• slab avalanches (cohesion due to sintering);
• wet-snow avalanches (cohesion due to capillarity).

Type of cohesion at release point	Avalanche type	Current names
Settling (Snow crystals linked by entanglement)		Powder-snow avalanche
Sintering (Snow crystals linked by ice bridges)		Slab avalanche (hard or soft)
Capillarity (Snow crystals linked by a film of water)		Wet-snow avalanche

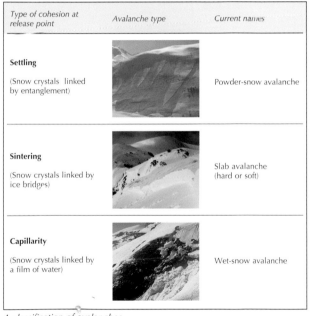

A classification of avalanches

This classification is quite basic, and although it is only an outline it gives information both on the circumstances of the release (time, cause) and on the characteristics of travel (speed, track).

Powder-snow Avalanches

A powder-snow avalanche is the flow of a snow layer of poor cohesion (settling). So these avalanches involve loose, dry snow, with low mass per volume. In other words, it is the kind of snow which will not form a snowball, which is very easy to ski and which crumbles into your tracks.

Powder-snow avalanches generally release from a single point. The avalanche rapidly grows in size as it runs, metre by metre. Seen from a distance, the track of these avalanches is often pear-shaped, particularly when they happen on a wide slope.

If the slope is steep and long, an airborne powder avalanche may develop. Otherwise the flow will take place on the surface: we call this a new snow slide.

New snow slides

The conditions which produce powder-snow avalanches are fairly typical. They are likely to take place on steep slopes and are usually seen during or immediately after snowfalls when the temperature is particularly low. They are much more frequent when the new snow is deposited on 'good' sliding bases, such as ice crusts.

As long as the speed of flow and the mass of snow are not too great, then this type of avalanche does not pose a real threat to the skier. However, an insignificant slide may become much bigger after a few dozen metres. If an airborne powder avalanche forms, the speed of the front of the avalanche often exceeds 200km/hr, which leaves the skier little chance of escape, particularly as the avalanche can travel over shallow-angled slopes or even, sometimes, climb the opposite slope over a distance of several hundred metres!

Although the deposits of snow debris in the run-out zones are rarely very big, airborne powder avalanches can cause great damage over considerable areas, mainly because of their notorious 'air-blast'.

Airborne powder avalanche: the snow clouds may develop to a height of several dozen metres

An airborne powder avalanche may run over shallow-angled slopes (here the slope is less than 20°)

Slab Avalanches

These avalanches, which are common at higher altitudes, are those which kill most winter mountain users.

A slab is a snow layer with relatively good cohesion, so that a fracture may spread over a whole mountain-side. In some ways, a slab release resembles a window breaking: in a fraction of a second, the whole slab breaks off, then disintegrates as it slides downhill.

A slab crownwall

The geometry of a slab varies widely. Its depth may vary from 10 centimetres to several metres; the width from a few metres to several kilometres. The characteristics of the snow also vary. Some slabs are soft and brittle, while others are hard and compact; some are of dry snow, while others are composed of damp or wet snow. So, on the mountains, slabs are difficult to recognise and locate.

A slab avalanche, as a rule, leaves little chance of escape for the person who triggers it. Very often, the fracture occurs well above the victim and the whole slope starts sliding at once.

Depending on size, the type of snow involved and the topography of the slide path, the slab breaks up more or less as it falls.

When the slab is very brittle and snow is dry, an airborne-powder avalanche may develop. When the slab is hard, the snow blocks slide or roll on the surface at moderate speeds (a few tens of km/hr) to the bottom of the slope, where they pile up in a chaotic mess.

The deposit of a slab avalanche

Snow which may appear powdery can produce a slab avalanche. This avalanche triggered spontaneously in the winter of 1987 on the Grand Sablat glacier (Grande Rousses range, France), on a south-east aspect after a major wind transport episode.

The depth of this particularly uniform slab varied from two to five metres

A skier can be very insignificant compared to some slabs as this L'Alpe d'Huez ski patroller jokingly illustrates

Wet-snow Avalanches

These avalanches often occur in the spring time, but are possible at any time during the winter. They follow on from thaws, rain or prolonged strong sunshine.

These weather conditions warm the snow and cause it to melt, thus moistening the snowpack. When the volume of water contained in the snowpack passes a certain threshold, its stability decreases considerably. The water promotes the melting of the bonds between the snow crystals on the one hand and lubricates the possible slide planes on the other.

Wet-snow avalanches typically exhibit a single-point release. The avalanche often begins as a small surface slide which grows in size little by little to potentially end up being of gigantic proportions.

The snow involved in these avalanches is dense (its mass per volume varies from 200 to 500kg/m^3) and often very wet. Certain wet-snow avalanches show many of the characteristics of mud slides; the snow may therefore be quite easily channelled by terrain features, and as a result it is generally fairly easy to predict their path. On the other hand, it is very difficult to predict the exact moment of their release: a snowpack full of water may remain in equilibrium for several days before sudden failure.

Wet-snow avalanches which have scoured away the snowpack to ground level after a prolonged thaw

A typical wet-snow avalanche, which occurred during a hot and sunny spring day

Wet-snow avalanche channelled by the terrain. The depth of the deposit in the runout zone is around four metres.

Wet-snow avalanche following a failure in the snowpack at the site of a glide crack (similar to the one shown by the arrows). The depth of the deposit in the runout zone is around two metres.

PERSONAL ACCOUNTS

Avalanche at Verbier (Valais, Switzerland), December 1997

Off on a ski tour on a beautiful day, they would never have thought... A female skier was carried down. She recalls:

'We decided to go for a trip above Verbier, a place well known to us. The weather was fine and settled. There was plenty of snow; there was a little powder on the high tops. We were out just for some fresh air, to stretch our legs, without thinking about what might happen. Skis on, we headed for the summit...

On the way up, I was looking at the slope, thinking about where we would ski down. There were several possibilities. One slope seemed quite attractive. There were fresh snowboard tracks on it. We decided to put in our tracks right next to them.

We thought "We'll have a great run!" The sun was still shining. As we were leaving, my friend said to me "Wait, I'll go and have a look at the way down, to see where the best line is. Stay there."

When he had done this, I went on. At the summit the terrain was flat, then it steepened on down...

On the way up, it had seemed rather steep, but the snow makes it look less serious, it gives you a different perspective. I threw myself into the descent. I did three turns. At the moment when I came to the drop-off, I felt it go!

At that point, there was nothing I could do. The snow was sliding under my skis. I said to myself, "OK, try to keep standing up," but it was hopeless. I let myself go and I thought "I hope my skis won't get caught in the snow and pull me down." At another moment I said, "I must see if there is anything coming down on top of me." I turned round and looked. Nothing was coming. At least that was something. The snow was becoming heavy and I felt as though I was borne along by waves which were carrying me down into the basin below. My fear was that, when I arrived at the bottom, in the hollow, everything would come down on my head. But at last, everything settled down and I was able to get up. I looked up and said to myself, "Now, out of here!"

The slope had been skied just before, there were snowboard tracks everywhere...'

Avalanche at Haute-Nendaz (Valais, Switzerland) February 1970

Twenty years on, the memory is still fresh in the mind of this ski professional who miraculously escaped from the snow.

'It was 11 February 1970. After two days of quite heavy snow-fall, there was about 80 centimetres of new snow. I was training a group of young ski instructors. They needed to do some work in deep snow to discover the medium, which I had always loved and respected.

We went off into the forest because I thought that it was too dangerous elsewhere. It was a forest which I knew by heart and had been using for years, skiing all the little gullies. So I went in and at the top of quite a steep gully I said to the youngsters, "Listen, it's not safe there. I'll try a turn amongst the trees." I wanted to ski-cut the snow layer, thinking it would part beneath my skis. I started off, and I went into my turn quite fast. Clearly, it fractured, but not in the way I expected. All of a sudden, I found myself on top of a snow layer which was moving. I had the time to notice the fracture line above me and I remember seeing rhododendrons and blue-berries passing by. I saw trees below me and thought I might be able to catch onto a larch. But, just a metre from the tree, the avalanche sucked me in and I couldn't catch it. Then I quickly threw off my ski sticks and dived forward as though into water. I thought that there was nothing else to do. I knew the terrain perfectly and I was really afraid of killing myself against a tree.

I made myself as small as possible and crossed my arms in front of me like a diver. I heard the blows, but didn't feel them, and I hit a tree and another and another, like a piece of timber that a lumberjack fells into a ravine. All of a sudden, about 500m further down, the avalanche began to slow down. I said to myself "OK, it's fine. You're saved!"

When I stopped I was able to open my eyes and see where I was. But just then another mass of snow suddenly arrived from behind and above, covering me completely. My right foot was up against my back and my left leg was stretched out.

My first reaction was to push both fists forward, then I raised my left hand, hoping to get it out of the snow: with my right hand I managed to work a little space in front of my mouth. But after perhaps four or five seconds I was completely trapped. I found myself a prisoner as though wrapped up in plaster. I could just move the ends of the fingers on my left hand: they were touching a larch branch which had been broken off and carried down in the avalanche. So then, I said to myself, "Jacques, you've been taken, you're stuck: now calm down and try not to waste energy."

As I wasn't out alone, I expected to be found quickly and I succeeded in calming down. With my mouth stuck up against my anorak on my left arm, I managed to breathe a little air.

After a few minutes the instructors arrived but they were looking for me lower down, in the middle of the couloir. I wanted to say to them, "I'm here! Come up, come up!" I heard them getting organised. The oldest of them sent someone to alert the ski area. I could hear everything. It was as though I was with the group. And I could do absolutely nothing. I waited. I hoped that an avalanche dog would come and find me. The minutes passed: things went over and over in my mind: my whole life went past at high speed mingled with moments of despair, "What is going to happen if they don't find me? Am I going to die here while I'm perfectly OK and with no serious injuries?"

About twenty minutes later, one of the guys, coming down the gully to see if I was pinned against a tree, saw one of my ski sticks, which by complete chance, was lying just above me. Searching the spot he touched the larch branch which I could touch with my left hand. At that I shook the branch.

Although I managed to do this, I could hear sweet music in my head; I couldn't feel anything any more. I just realised that asphyxia was taking me away gently. I don't know where I found the incredible resources to shake that branch...

I immediately heard the guy shout, "He's here! It moved! He's here!" Then all his pals who were further down came back up and in minutes they had cleared my face, then dug me out of the snow.

Then I saw my brother arrive with the rescue sledge. I just had the time to smile and say to him, "I'm fine, I'll ski down; what are you doing with that thing there?" And then I collapsed.' *

*The final outcome of this accident was torn ligaments on the right knee, along with multiple abrasions.

Avalanche on Mont Mort (Grand Saint Bernard area, Switzerland, March 1991)

Jacky Michelet has devoted 30 years of his life to mountain rescue, first with the cantonal police in Valais, then in the FXB rescue organisation. He has participated in more than 700 rescues, particularly those resulting from avalanches. His personal account and thoughts are those of a highly experienced guide and rescuer.

'If you get out of an avalanche alive, it is due to huge good luck. Because most of the time avalanches kill. And even if rescue comes very quickly, the waiting time for victims struggling to survive is often too long.

All the avalanches I have seen have left me with a heavy burden.

I remember, for instance, an avalanche near the Col du St Bernard where seven people, mostly teenagers, lost their lives. They thought they were in a safe area. The weather was very bad. It was snowing and visibility was poor. In the afternoon two groups set off on an easy route. After the first group reached the summit, which was both groups' intended goal, and as they were descending, they passed the second group who were still coming up. The two group leaders conferred: it was windy, it was cold, there wasn't much to see but the snow was good. The first group carried on down to the hospice. The second group carried on in single file up a kind of gully protected behind a ridge.

Suddenly, the great Mont Mort avalanche released, leaving a crownwall four to five metres high. Unbelievable masses of snow came down and crashed against the ridge protecting the skiers. The snow was projected vertically into the air and fell back down on the group, completely burying them. Some of them were buried without even being knocked over.

The last skier in the group, who was unharmed, went back down very quickly to the hospice and raised the alarm. In no time at all the rescuers, along with an avalanche dog, were at the scene. But the outcome was tragic. This terrible story shows that there is no such thing as complete safety.

The Mont Mort Avalanche killed seven people on a route which seemed to be safe. After the accident, the Rector of the College of Lausanne told the press 'According to our recollections – and the oldest of us is 80 – there has never before been an avalanche at that place!'

Avalanche at Lourtier, February 1999

On Sunday, 21st February 1999, an avalanche struck the Valaisan village of Lourtier. Miraculously, no-one was killed. Gerald Maret, mountain guide and a resident in the village, tells us:

'I had never seen conditions like these since I was a child, when we could ski down to the village. Now we could ski down into the bottom of the valleys, every day bringing 20 to 30 cm or more of powder snow. We could even ski through the very densest forest. Then there was an avalanche which came down to just above the village. No-one had ever seen that before. Certainly not the young ones like me. Talking about it the older inhabitants said they had seen it before. But their memories didn't seem very clear on the subject.

It carried on snowing. It really was a big dump. On Friday 19th we still skied, with a group of friends. From Verbier we skied down to Chable; after that we went up to Bruson and we skied down to Sembrancher. It was really great. And then, at the end of the day, it began to rain. On our last run down to Sembrancher we got really wet. The snow was getting heavy. Rain, rain, rain! When I got up on Saturday morning, it was throwing it down. It was raining very high, up to the tree line.

We abandoned our plans for skiing and went home. There, I started to examine the situation.

I began to think that with the snow that had already fallen, the fact that it was still snowing up high and with the rain, things were becoming dangerous. And already in the village, there were two or three people who were preparing to leave to go and stay elsewhere or to spend the night elsewhere. They would come back during the day, but would sleep elsewhere at night. Everyone felt that something was going to happen.

That day two avalanches occurred up at the bridge in the village. They stopped 10 or 15 metres from the bridge, but the depth of the debris was higher than the bridge. Everyone in the valley came to see it. The people living round about were frightened. Nobody knew what to do.

It rained all Saturday and through the night into Sunday. And on Sunday it carried on. The authorities debated whether or not to evacuate. The villagers became more and more apprehensive. About two or three in the afternoon there was another avalanche. Then there was the avalanche at five o'clock, which was really big and which crossed the bridge, destroying a garage and a house, and reached the dairy and the chapel. It cut the village in two. Then panic broke out. And still, the weather continued. I was at home; I had just realised that there had been an avalanche because everyone was shouting when it came down. I went to see. A house had disappeared beneath it. People were running everywhere. The decision had been made to evacuate the village. People from all over the village were clambering over the avalanche which had come down in order to get away. And then there was another avalanche alert!

We were in the bistrot, organising the evacuation. We heard "Avalanche, avalanche!" We went outside. We heard shouting and could see the whole forest breaking up. There was a noise of grinding metal. The electricity pylons were coming down. There had been a terrific rainfall, like a monsoon. And we saw the front of the avalanche coming. It was five or six metres high, was following the road and was coming slowly. It was 20 metres away from us. We ran before it, we stopped, we ran again. Cars were being crushed all around. The avalanche followed the road for 200 to 300m, then stopped. We didn't know if the houses in the village were still standing. It was seven o'clock at night. It was dark.'

The volume of snow which hit the village of Lourtier, 21 February 1999, was very substantial. Miraculously, no-one was hurt.

A few hours after the Lourtier avalanche, another hit the village of Évolène, in the Val d'Hérens. It carried away several chalets and killed 12 people. The weather conditions before these exceptionally large avalanches were characterised by very heavy snowfalls accompanied by strong winds, followed by thaw with rain. These conditions explain the unusual volume of these avalanches, which showed large airborne powder development while still involving considerable quantities of dense snow running on the surface.

The volumes of snow deposited in the run-out zones were impressive, several hundred thousand cubic metres, with a depth of 25m! Mixed flows like this are extremely destructive.

The avalanche at Évolène killed 12 people and caused severe material damage

Avalanches at Arinsal, February 1996

Avalanches ravage areas other than the Alps. In 1996 Arinsal, in the Andorran Pyrenees, was the scene of an exceptionally large avalanche. Jean-Francois Meffre, head of the avalanche safety service in Andorra, tells the story.

'At the end of January 1996 Andorra was covered in a thick blanket of snow (1.5–2m at 2000m altitude). The 60cm of fresh snow which fell on 21 January was followed by a series of snow-falls which, although not heavy, sufficed to slow down the consolidation of the snowpack. At the start of February, a north-east airflow brought a series of depressions. On the 5 February, 20cm of snow fell at Arinsal, followed by 50cm on the 6th. After a brief respite, the storm returned on the morning of the 7th. The wind was blowing at 100km/hr at 3000m. The squalls of snow stopped all vehicular traffic in the high valleys of Andorra. The

snowploughs had to stop work. The villagers had not seen such a quantity of snow for a very long time. The Col d'Envalira (2400m) was clearly impassable. The villages of Serrat and Cannilo were cut off. The access roads to the ski resorts of Solden and Arcalis were blocked. During the night of the 7th to 8th the storm raged; large avalanches released, particularly on south and south-west aspects. Around five o'clock in the morning, a large powder avalanche, which released at 2700m on the south face of Les Planes, swept across the car park at Arcalis, which was empty and closed to the public.

The size of this event persuaded the avalanche safety service to evacuate a group of buildings at the bottom of the Arinsal valley, which lies below a large cirque of the same orientation as the recent avalanche. The operation involved more than 300 people. It was difficult to get hold of responsible authorities before nine o'clock; the decision was only taken around 10 o'clock. Several buildings constructed in the 1980s were directly exposed to the les Fonts avalanche path and their access road was threatened over a distance of several hundred metres by three slide paths.

The first couloir (Percanela) confirmed our fears around 10.30am: an avalanche cut the only road over a width of 100m. Fortunately, no-one was buried: the roadway, covered to a depth of four metres by a mixture of snow and broken trees, could neither be cleared nor negotiated. The evacuation of the buildings was seriously held up; people had to take a detour, transported in tracked vehicles from the ski area, then descend on foot across a building site to the coaches, which were waiting on the other side of the avalanche. The fire service and police accompanied the villagers and tourists in small groups. There was no panic, but there was some argument as many people wanted to take away as many belongings as possible. At 5.30pm the evacuation was complete; two police officers stood guard 500m from the avalanche couloir to prevent access to the danger zone. At 7pm, they heard a noise like a hurricane and the cracking of broken trees; then the air-blast pushed their big 4 x 4 vehicle 10 metres across the carriageway.

The air-blast blew over the old village of Arinsal and was still felt more than a kilometre from the couloir. The mountain had been forgiving once more: it had waited until everyone had got away!

At daybreak, the full scale of the damage became visible: it was extensive! It was like arriving after a bombing raid or an immense tornado. Eight of the 12 buildings evacuated had been damaged by the avalanche. The hundreds of trees carried down by the avalanche had acted as battering rams. Brick walls had exploded, only concrete walls and some natural stone ones had survived. The snow had gone right through some buildings, depositing furniture and rubble at the bottom of the exterior walls, even tearing out electrical fittings.

The roof of a six-storey building, on the river bank opposite the couloir, was torn off and half of its picture windows and partition walls had been smashed to pieces. The depth of snow made it possible to enter the building on foot at the second floor. Several weeks later, we discovered that the floor of the first storey at the centre of the building had been pushed up to the ceiling of the second storey (it came down gently as the snow melted).

With the air-blast, vehicles in the car park had been crushed; others were blown along to the first pylons of the chairlift. Windscreens were shattered, vehicles filled with snow. The only buildings to survive undamaged were two small ones with avalanche-shedding roofs, tucked into the slope amongst the rocks.

This avalanche followed a known path (hence the evacuation) but there had not been such a large one in living memory. The old folks in the valley could recall previous events. After the last war, a wet-snow avalanche had travelled across fields to the river bottom. Another time, it had stopped just at the foot of the water-fall. The most recent avalanche, at the start of the '60s, was the biggest; it emptied out the whole cirque and spread itself on the meadows across the river. The debris completely filled the river, but it was no more than 70 metres wide according to aerial photographs.

In 1996, its track through the forest was twice as wide!'

The roof of this six-storey building was torn off by the avalanche

Here, the avalanche destroyed every apartment

Risk Assessment

DEFINITION OF RISK

Avalanches cause damage which may be considerable and which may involve infrastructure (buildings, vehicles, equipment, ski lifts, communication routes, etc.), the environment (forests and lakes), as well as living creatures.

Buildings damaged by avalanches

Damage caused in the forest of Arbaz (Valais), in February 1999, by an avalanche started in the Sionne valley: it will take several decades for this scar to heal.

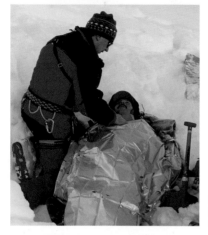

In Europe there are at least 100 avalanche victims every year.

An avalanche can smash a chalet to pieces

The destructive power of an avalanche depends, on the one hand, on the volumetric mass of the moving snow, and, on the other, on the speed of its movement*.

The pressure exerted on obstacles in the path of the avalanche can be colossal (several hundred kPa) and the snow may sweep all before it!

✔ *There is no risk unless there is a possibility of damage.*

---

* *Static pressure = $f(P, v^2)$*

Very often, risk is wrongly assumed to be the probability of a given event occurring. So, in popular language, one might easily say that there is a risk of rain because the sky is covering over with black clouds. But this verbal shorthand should not make us forget that risk depends not only on the probability that the event will occur, but also on the consequences of this possible event. While climbing a ladder, the risk you are taking increases rung by rung, even though the probability of falling remains the same!

In very general terms, therefore, risk depends on a probability and on a susceptibility to harm. In order to make a valid assessment of a risk, whatever it may be, one must evaluate both. The same applies to assessing avalanche risk.

To evaluate an avalanche risk, it is necessary to estimate the probability that an avalanche will occur and also to assess the consequences of this hypothetical avalanche.

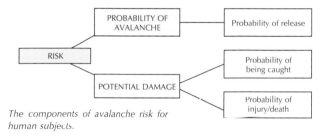

The components of avalanche risk for human subjects.

✔ It is essential to remember that it is not enough just to look at the snow in order to make an avalanche risk assessment!

On the other hand, to make a proper analysis, it is not enough to take into account only injury to your self. It is also important to estimate the jeopardy in which you may be placing other people by causing material or bodily damage. Risk should therefore be evaluated by considering globally the potential jeopardy (see table on following page).

As we see, it is fundamental to make the distinction between avalanche risk and the probability of avalanche in order to make a correct assessment and adopt suitable responses!

	Potential Damage		
Avalanche Probability ▼	Personal bodily injury - No bodily injury to others - No material damage	Personal bodily injury - No bodily injury to others - Material damage	Personal bodily injury - Bodily injury to others - Material damage
Considerable or High	High Risk	Very High Risk	Extreme Risk
Low	Moderate Risk	High Risk	Very High Risk
Very Low	Reduced Risk	Moderate Risk	High Risk

Avalanche risk – a function of two independent components: avalanche probability and potential damage

The problem of assessing avalanche risk, even when addressed properly, is still complex, principally because of the difficulty in estimating avalanche probability. Avalanche bulletins issued by official sources can provide certain assistance and must therefore always be consulted. In Europe, these bulletins use a hazard scale consisting of five levels, from 'Low Hazard' to 'Very High Hazard'. These bulletins are very useful – if they are used wisely. It should be remembered that the bulletin indicates an average hazard level for areas which may be several hundred square kilometres in extent. But, the hazard level is very variable from one slope to another and from one moment to another. At hazard level three, for instance, some areas my be perfectly safe, while others may be extremely hazardous.

✔ *Taking note of bulletins is essential, but is not adequate for making local risk assessments and is not a substitute for making your own careful observations.*

Lastly, it is worth noting that risk is constant only for a certain place and time: a risk can only be evaluated for a particular geographical area and a given time interval. In other words, one needs constantly to repeat these evaluations, as one moves around and as time passes. Basic rule: always stay **receptive** and **reactive**.

European Avalanche Hazard Scale

Degree of Hazard	Snowpack Stability	Avalanche Probability
1: Low	The snowpack is generally well bonded and stable.	Triggering is possible only with high additional loads (e.g. a group of skiers) on a few very steep extreme slopes. Only a few small natural avalanches (sluffs) possible.
2: Moderate	The snowpack is moderately well bonded on some steep slopes, otherwise generally well bonded.	Triggering is possible with high additional loads, particularly on the steep slopes indicated in the bulletin. Large natural avalanches not likely.
3: Considerable	The snowpack is moderately to weakly bonded on many steep slopes.	Triggering is possible, sometimes even with low additional loads. The bulletin may indicate many slopes which are particularly affected. In certain conditions, medium and occasionally large sized natural avalanches may occur.
4: High	The snowpack is weakly bonded in most places.	Triggering is probable even with low additional loads on many steep slopes. In some conditions, frequent medium or large sized natural avalanches are likely.
5: Very High	The snowpack is generally weakly bonded and largely unstable.	Numerous large natural avalanches are likely, even on moderately steep terrain.

CRITERIA FOR RISK ASSESSMENT

In assessing risk, it is useful to make separate analyses of the two components – avalanche probability and potential damage.

Avalanche Probability

An avalanche releases when the forces acting upon the snow-pack exceed the strength and friction which resist the fracture and movement of the snow. Thus any factor which tends to increase these forces and reduce strength or friction becomes a criterion for the assessment of avalanche probability.

The probability of avalanche increases particularly:
- with the accumulation of water (rain, melting) or snow (precipitation or drifting)
- with the overloading (cornice or serac fall, skier on slope, etc.)
- with the angle of the slope
- if the snow has poor cohesion (snow saturated with water, weak layers)
- if the bond between layers is poor (graupel, surface hoar)
- if sliding surfaces exist (smooth soil, buried crusts).

Some of these criteria, like slope angle or the presence of anchoring features, for example, are clearly observable in the field. Others, such as the quality of the bonds between layers, are less obvious. These factors are more readily understood by studying associated meteorological events which are easier to observe.

Potential Damage

It seems impossible, *a priori*, to determine whether someone will survive an avalanche or not. In reality, one can assume nothing regarding the injuries which someone may suffer, nor the efficiency of rescue attempts, nor the victim's will to live. In addition, to err on the side of caution (because people often lose their lives in insignificant slides), potential damage is assessed below mainly based on the probability of the victim being carried down and, along with this, the probability of being rescued.

The probability of being carried down depends on:
- the characteristics of the release (position and size of starting zone)
- the characteristics of the flow (snow mass, speed, trajectory)
- the local topography
- the mobility of the group.

The probability of rescue depends on:
- the weather and snow conditions
- local geography
- the group self-sufficiency in rescue equipment.

Note: assuming that no-one will consider action which might harm other people, we will consider only the risk to the individual.

✔ *If following a route or making a ski descent could endanger other people then there is no point in deliberating on the stability of the snowpack: the route must simply be avoided. The mountains are big enough to offer other possibilities.*

Article 223-1 of the French Penal Code:
'the act of directly exposing others to an immediate risk of death or injury such as to lead to permanent mutilation or disability through the manifestly deliberate breach of a particular requirement of safety and care required by the law or regulation is punishable by one year in prison and a fine of 15,000 euros.'

Food for Thought...

In 1997, in a French ski resort, two snowboarders went onto a black run which was closed with ropes and warning notices. They triggered a release which fortunately did not reach the ski patrollers who were working below. Two days later, one of them took the same run, still closed. Charged with deliberately endangering the lives of others, they were both convicted in the first instance by the criminal court. The Court of Appeal confirmed the sentence, while increasing that of the recidivist: the culprits were given fines of 6000 and 8000 francs respectively. In addition, the verdict was published in two local newspapers and posted on notice boards in the ski resort at the expense of the convicted persons. This decision was confirmed by the High Court in 1999.*

Avalanche Risk

In the final analysis, avalanche probability and potential damage both vary with:

- local weather and snow conditions
- the terrain (route taken)
- the group.

✔ *The assessment of avalanche risk must always include these three factors.*

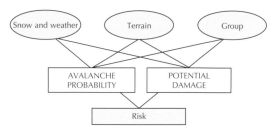

Types of information required for assessment of avalanche risk

---

* *Source: National Association for Snow and Avalanche Studies (ANENA), Grenoble*

The replies to the following questions will allow a better analysis of the local situation and will provide criteria for the assessment of avalanche risk (see following pages).

Snow and Weather		Has it rained in the past two days? Has there been snowfall in the past three days? Has there been wind transport of snow in the past five days? What is the air temperature? Is there poor visibility?
		Is there (very) deep snow? Is there wet snow? Is the snowpack uneven (depth or layering)? Are there snow pillows or cornices? Is there an internal weak layer?
		Are there avalanches occurring today? Were there avalanches yesterday or the day before? Are there cracks in the snowpack?
Terrain		Is the route without shelter (islands of safety, etc)? Is the route exposed (rock tiers, crevasses, seracs)? Is it an unfrequented route? Is it a route with steep slopes? Is it a route with steep slopes above? Are there steep convex slopes?
Group		Do members of the group lack the normal technical skills? Are there members of the group in poor physical condition? Are all members of the group carrying a transceiver, probe and shovel? Does the group consist of more than five or less than three people? Has the group received rescue training?

Note: If all slopes in the area are below 25°, or completely covered in thick forest (too dense to ski), or if there is a general cover of strong melt-freeze crust, then the probability of avalanche release may be assumed to be more or less nil.

We will now review each of these risk factors in more detail.

 Furrows in the snow surface. Snow surface compacted, sometimes with a texture like orange peel. Water present in the snow.

Rain in
the Past Two Days

Drainage of water added to the snowpack by rain is neither complete nor instantaneous. So, just after rain, the snow may contain large quantities of water in retention or in transit. With the resulting increase in weight, the possibility of fracture increases. Moreover the water weakens bonding and reduces friction: and if water percolating down through the snowpack encounters a layer which is impermeable or already saturated (an ice layer, for example) it can even act as a lubricating agent.

Therefore, many avalanches occur during heavy rain, particularly if this follows immediately on from heavy snowfall. These avalanches are channelled by the terrain and follow predictable paths. However, very many slopes may be affected at the same time, which sometimes makes it difficult to turn back. As a rule, this extreme activity is short-lived (one to two days) and is often as brief as it is intense. It should be noted that this instability only occurs when rain follows snowfall or when the snowpack is already saturated.

In case of recent heavy rain
Avalanche probability: (greatly) increased
Potential damage: +/- unchanged

🔍 Trees and cables still snowed up. Snow surface shining (high albedo). With dry snow: ski tracks soft, closing up. Stellar crystals may be seen on the snow surface. Relatively few animal tracks. Snow grooming in process.

Snowfall in
the Past Three Days

Statistics and experience show that the number of spontaneous or triggered avalanches is higher during and just after most significant snowfalls (more than 20 centimetres). This is because the changes which may lead to the consolidation of the new snow layers and their adhesion to under-lying layers take place only progressively: so bonding between the new crystals remains dubious for a certain time (several hours to several days). It is also noticeable that avalanches occur-ring after snowfall involve only the recently fallen snow in their starting zones.

The probability of spontaneous release grows with the depth of new snow and particularly with the intensity of the snowfall. It diminishes as the snow gains in cohesion, in contrast to the probability of triggered avalanches, which may remain high, particularly if the bond with underlying layers is poor (melt-freeze crust) or if these are fragile (buried surface hoar, graupel).

The snow crystals are then sufficiently well bonded to each other to produce slab avalanches under the additional load and may even be trig-gered from some distance away.

In case of recent snow
Avalanche probability: (greatly) increased
Potential damage: +/- unchanged

 Plumes of wind-blown snow. Snow surface showing micro-relief which is quite soft; wrinkles, waves, raised tracks. Snow pillows at breaks of slope. Ridges showing well-defined cornices. Rounded tops stripped of snow. Marked local variations in snow depth. Tree trunks and steep cliffs plastered with snow. Roofs unevenly loaded.

Wind Transport
of Snow in the Past Five Days

In the mountains the wind regularly moves large quantities of snow from exposed areas to sheltered spots. This transfer, which goes on during and after snowfall, generally results in a reduction in the size of transported snow particles, which favours their bonding by sintering after deposition. So a layer of wind-deposited snow has a certain cohesion, reducing the probability of spontaneous release, but permitting, on the other hand, the possibility of a fracture due to localised over-loading. This is the legendary 'wind-slab'.

These layers stay unstable as long as they are poorly bonded to the base layer, which may be several days at least: after a wind transport episode, the probability of triggering an avalanche is therefore higher, and when one is triggered the chances of escape are slim because the victim is normally surrounded by a chaotic mass of blocks in motion. Beware! This latent instability can persist for a long time, especially if the wind-deposited snow lies on a fragile layer which metamorphoses slowly (buried surface hoar, graupel). However, this tends to be localised.

In case of recent wind transport
Avalanche probability: (greatly) increased
Potential damage: increased

 Flows and weeps of water. Snow more or less sticky, heavy and wet. Snow has fallen or is falling from trees. Visibility often poor. Cumuliform clouds possibly forming. Vegetation flowering.

Positive Air Temperature

We tend to say that spontaneous avalanches, besides these occurring during snowfall, take place most often in 'warm' weather, at times of winter thaw or in the spring. But this judgement does not directly link cause to effect; the consequences of heat vary greatly according to the state of the snowpack: in general, it will stabilise powder snow, while it will increase the instability of saturated layers, sometimes causing large full-depth avalanches.

If the temperature is positive, it does not necessarily follow that the snowpack is unstable. On the other hand, when avalanches occur because of high temperatures, it is possible to conclude that many neighbouring slopes of similar altitude will be implicated at the same time. If the route being followed becomes impracticable, other nearby routes will also be! The walker or ski-tourer can therefore be trapped, with no exit. So, it is mainly because warm weather can occasionally lead to generalised instability and spontaneous avalanches that it appears as a risk factor.

In case of positive air temperature
Probability of avalanche: increased
Potential damage: increased

Cloud, blizzard, very heavy snowfall, night – visibility can change from one moment to another (A), but also from one place to another (B).

**Poor
Visibility**

Visibility determines avalanche risk to some extent because in the case of an accident, it affects the probability of finding the victim quickly and therefore the chances of survival. In poor visibility, searching is more difficult, the deployment of rescue teams is often delayed or even impossible and the evacuation of the victim takes longer, especially if helicopters are unable to fly. Visibility also affects indirectly the probability of triggering an avalanche. For, when it is not possible to see more than a few metres, it is very difficult to detect suspect zones, particularly as the senses tend to be very confused (in mist, it is possible to fall over standing still when you think you are moving (or vice versa! – trans)). Moreover, sometimes the party has to regroup in case someone gets lost or in order to navigate by compass. But a snowpack which will support the passage of several people one at a time may fail if they are all in one group, thereby creating high overload.

Finally, lack of visibility increases the possibility of being struck by an avalanche from above, leaving no chance of escape – the front of the avalanche as well as any possible shelter being invisible.

Beware! Visibility changes very quickly in the mountains.

In case of poor visibility
Avalanche probability: increased
Potential damage: greatly increased

 Deep foot penetration. Deep ski tracks. Terrain features covered over.

(Very)
Deep Snow

Snow is said to be 'deep' when a walker penetrates 20 to 40 centimetres into it, and 'very deep' if the walker sinks in more than 40 centimetres.

There are several kinds of deep snow, from new snow, wet or dry, of varying density, to very dense old snow. In all cases, the depth of penetration of a walker gives an indication of the minimum depth of un-stabilised snow at the surface of the snow-pack.

When this snow has no cohesion, the lateral, uphill and downslope anchorages are more or less inoperative. The equilibrium of the snowpack then depends essentially on the constraint due to its own weight and on its resistance to shearing. So, there exist for each slope critical depths of new snow beyond which an avalanche may start spontaneously: skiers are then threatened by the natural release of slopes above.

If the snow possesses some cohesion, it may accumulate in greater quantities. In this case, the skier must beware of avalanches triggered by the loading he or she places on the snowpack. The risk may be high, as these avalanches (brittle slab fractures) may be of great size.

In case of (very) deep snow
Avalanche probability: greatly increased
Potential damage: increased

 Dull-coloured snow, with big round agglomerations of grains, sometimes reminiscent of thick porridge. Snow surface wrinkled on steep slopes. Snowballs leave the hand wet. Difficult skiing. Poor jerky sliding properties. Rivers full.

Wet Snow

The presence of water within the snowpack following rain or a long period of warm and/or sunny weather influences its stability. With low liquid water content, the bonding of the grains by capillarity gives fair cohesion of the snowpack. However, if there is a high liquid water content, this capillary cohesion becomes much weaker, and this leads to the de-stabilisation of the snowpack.

If the water content results from rain, avalanches will occur almost immediately on a variety of slopes. Then one has a kind of 'spate' of avalanches. On the other hand, if the water content results from good spring weather, the avalanche releases are less immediate and more spread out. The steepest and most exposed slopes are the first to go, sometimes around the end of the morning.

So it can be seen that wet snow is not necessarily unstable. It only becomes so when a certain threshold of wetness is exceeded. Sadly, in the field it is quite difficult to determine that! It is best to be suspicious of wet snow, particularly on big, steep, uniform open slopes.

In case of wet snow
Avalanche probability: (greatly) increased
Potential damage: increased

Very variable snow depth with a fairly small average depth (less than a metre): resistance to penetration of a ski stick changes from one place to another; sudden alterations in ski penetration. Variable sliding properties: snow surface characteristics very varied; big differences in the brightness of the snow on a given slope.

Uneven Snowpack

After the snow has gone, it is sometimes surprising to find rough ground where, in winter, the terrain seemed to be smooth and regular. The snow does not always follow the ground exactly, and sometimes the properties of the snowpack change considerably over short distances. We know, for instance, that on a uniform slope, the depth of the snow at one spot can sometimes be twice that at another close by!

Significant changes of the snow surface are often accompanied by variations in its depth or in its internal structure, which may lead, if the variations are large, to great inhomogeneity in stability from one place to another. So, it is difficult to assess the risk without good local knowledge, notably of the topography and recent avalanche activity.

To choose a safe route through an uneven snowpack therefore requires considerable experience, particularly if the snowpack is shallow.

In case of an uneven snowpack
Avalanche probability: increased
Potential damage: +/- unchanged

A. Snow pillows: snow deposits behind terrain features, sometimes looking like sand dunes, can range from about 20 centimetres to several metres deep.

B and C. Cornices are accumulations on ridges, sometimes forming overhangs.

Snow Pillows or Cornices

Snow pillows or cornices are the most obvious evidence of wind transport of snow. They are particularly easy to observe and give valuable information on local conditions. They are especially good indicators of redistribution of snow on the ground – and so of the deposition of large accumulations (well known as windslab) – on lee slopes and sometimes also on windward slopes. These slabs, which are very difficult to locate before they fracture, can be huge (several metres deep over an area of several hectares) and always constitute a danger to life.

So cornices and snow pillows should always be regarded as serious alarm signals, particularly if they are freshly formed (when they are recognisable by their relative lack of stratification and their angular forms).

Some avalanches are triggered by cornice collapses. So a cornice is not only a risk factor, but a real hazard in itself.

In case of snow pillows or cornices
Avalanche probability: greatly increased
Potential damage: increased

🔍 On the surface: snow crystals with the appearance of frost 'leaves'. Within the snowpack angular snow crystals, flowing through the fingers like sugar. Discontinuity between two similar layers (only observable by performing a shear test).

Internal
Weak Layer

Weak layers are snow strata with poor cohesion, which become of great concern when they are buried. Their very poor shear strength facilitates the failure and sliding of the layers above them; they are like piles of grit on roads which give way under your wheels.

These layers may form for different reasons. Sometimes they are of rounded crystals (graupel), whose large spherical shapes do not bond well with each other; at other times, they are of surface hoar, like crushed ice. But most often, these layers are formed by snow metamorphism resulting from a strong vertical temperature gradient within the snowpack, leading to the formation of angular grains (see pp5–6), then 'cup crystals' with no bonding between them. In all cases, fragile layers do not metamorphose much and will persist until a thorough wetting of the snowpack occurs.

The fragile internal layers are difficult to make out because they are buried, but also because they are often thin (sometimes only a few millimetres thick). However, they often form at times of hail showers, freezing fogs or on shaded slopes after a long cold clear period, and caution should be exercised in these conditions.

In case of internal weak layer
Avalanche probability: (greatly) increased
Potential damage: +/- unchanged

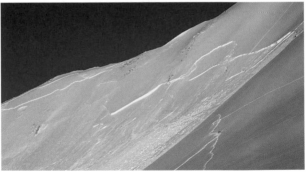

 Fractures still angular. Snow deposits are still soft in the case of dry-snow avalanches. Animal tracks are covered up. Roads blocked by avalanche are still not cleared.

Avalanches on the Day

It is evident that avalanches often happen in epidemics, in fairly short periods lasting from a few hours to a few days. Generally, one avalanche is the precursor of others.

The fact that an avalanche has occurred during a given day overrides all previous theorising and shows that the snowpack is, at least locally, unstable. As it is likely that snow and topographical conditions similar to those which have produced the observed avalanche will exist in other places in the same mountain range, this event should be seen as a real alarm signal.

If the avalanche is a result of rain, thaw or snowfalls, unaccompanied by wind, then all slopes of the same altitude and angle to the one where the avalanche happened should be considered highly suspect, especially if the avalanches are spontaneous. In other cases, one should be cautious about drawing general conclusions about the location of unstable areas. In fact after an episode of wind transport, avalanches are frequently seen at differing altitudes and slope aspects.

In the case of avalanches on the day
Avalanche probability: greatly increased
Potential damage: +/- unchanged

Fractures still evident, but deposits already compacting.

Avalanche
Yesterday or the Day Before

An avalanche which has occurred in the preceding days can indicate two types of hazardous situation. If the avalanche follows a snowfall or a wind transport episode, it provides evidence of a former instability which may still persist! In this case, some slopes will be safe, while others, even very close by, may be unstable. This instability may persist for several days, which may easily thwart the vigilance of the most careful observer.

If the observed avalanche is due to spring sunshine, an increase in instability and in the number of avalanches is to be expected as the day goes on – the steepest slopes at lower altitudes and with a south-easterly aspect being the most likely locations. When there is a strong re-freezing overnight, the hazard seems to start from about midday. But when overnight freezing is weak or absent, the instability may by evident in the morning. In the spring, therefore, it is wise to be very careful after a cloudy night following a period of fine, sunny weather, and it should be remembered that an early start is not an absolute guarantee of safety. On the other hand, a late start, particularly on a south-facing route, is definitely unwise.

In case of an avalanche yesterday or the day before
Avalanche probability: increased
Potential damage: unchanged

A. In dry snow: thin cracks rarely exceed a few metres and are difficult to see.

B and C. In wet snow: wide cracks, down to ground level, may be several metres wide and several tens of metres in length.

Cracks
in the Snowpack

A crack in the snowpack results from a tension fracture and indicates that the equilibrium of the snowpack depends entirely on its resistance to shearing and compression. So one may conclude, *a priori*, that its stability is diminished. Nevertheless, two very different situations may be distinguished.

Cracks in dry snow, sometimes accompanied by loud 'whumpfing' sounds, generally indicate extreme instability. They show that the snow is cohesive enough to form a slab, but probably insufficiently cohesive to guarantee its stability in case of additional loading.

Cracks in wet snow occur when snow creep is rapid. They show a decrease in friction at the base of the snowpack, so that its equilibrium depends mainly on its downslope anchorage and its resistance to compression. The last is generally quite good for dense snow, and the snowpack is not necessarily unstable when cracks of this kind appear. It is, moreover, quite common for avalanches not to happen until several days after the appearance of these cracks, or perhaps not at all. But avalanche probability increases as the snowpack becomes wetter, and may end up by being high.

In case of cracks in the snow
Avalanche probability: (greatly) increased
Potential damage: +/- unchanged

Wide, open slopes, uniformly angled, with no large rocks sticking through or well-defined ridges (A. route with no shelter; B. route with shelter).

**Routes
Without Shelter**

Although there are many avalanche paths in the mountains there are also many areas where avalanches do not occur and which therefore constitute natural shelters. These take many different forms: extensive flat areas, large erratic boulders, promontories, moraines... A route with natural shelter makes it possible to proceed from one island of safety to another, restricting the number of people exposed to danger at the same time. In case of avalanche, the chances of escape are better, and in the worst scenario, the number of persons carried down will be reduced and the number of rescuers (those who haven't been carried down!) is increased. Moreover, broken slopes are less likely to produce big avalanches involving the whole slope. For given snow conditions, therefore, a slope without shelter is *per se* more hazardous, particularly for large groups.

But not all shelter is safe. Isolated trees or small boulders, for instance, do not provide adequate shelter, and in general islands of safety become rare when large avalanches are likely to release, particularly if airborne powder avalanches occur.

In case of route without shelter
Avalanche probability: +/- unchanged
Potential damage: greatly increased

🔍 Rock tiers, cliffs, mixed ground, bergschrunds, crevasses, seracs, gorges, rivers and lakes.

**Exposed Route
(rock tiers, crevasses, seracs)**

The snowpack on a slope above a cliff or a bergschrund is more or less deprived of support on its downslope side: its stability is, by the same token, more dubious. In case of avalanche, the chances of escape may be limited or non-existent, and, crucially, the victim may be carried over a cliff or down onto rocks, even by an insignificant slide. The risk of serious injury is high – in an area where a rescue may be difficult to achieve.

If the victim is carried down into a crevasse or ends up against the bottom of a cliff, he or she may be deeply buried by the following mass of snow: the victim may be difficult to find (probes may be too short or not strong enough) and to dig out (the snow will often be extremely compacted).

Exposed routes always present a problem. It is well worth thinking twice before setting out and, if possible, making a scrupulous prior reconnaissance, for return or retreat will often be impossible.

In case of an exposed route
Avalanche probability: increased
Potential damage: greatly increased

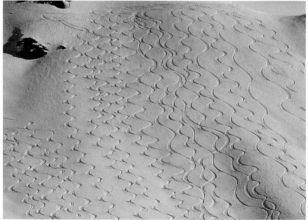

Examples of well-frequented routes

 No tracks even after several days of fine weather following snowfall.

Unfrequented Route

Regular heavy traffic on a route causes a certain degree of stabilisation. Effectively the repeated passage of skis or feet leads to compacting of the snow. This increases the cohesion of recently fallen snow, provides bonding between layers and acts against the formation of weak layers composed of depth hoar or buried surface hoar. Multiple intersecting tracks create roughnesses, improving the cohesion of fresh snow layers, particularly if the tracked-out snow has started to stabilise. So, the heavier and more frequent the traffic, the more the likelihood of avalanche release will diminish.

This packing effect will also tend to limit the size of potential avalanches, which will often only involve the surface layers of the snowpack, showing single point release.

On an unfrequented route, this kind of stabilisation does not take place. Moreover, in the case of an accident, immediate outside help cannot be expected; if the site is very remote, organised rescue may not quickly be available. The consequence of an avalanche may therefore be more serious.

On an unfrequented route
Avalanche probability: increased
Potential damage: increased

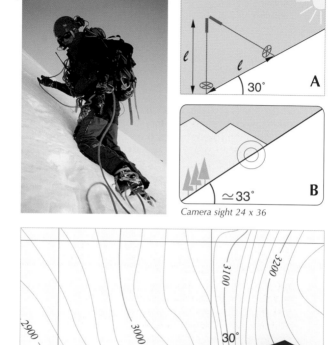

Camera sight 24 x 36

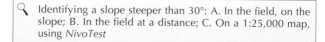

Identifying a slope steeper than 30°: A. In the field, on the slope; B. In the field at a distance; C. On a 1:25,000 map, using *NivoTest*

Route with Steep Slopes

Gravity is the engine of the avalanche: the steeper the slope and the greater the downslope traction forces acting upon it (due to its own weight), the more likely it is for the snowpack to fracture and slide. The traction created by a single skier is stronger on a steep slope: for instance, it is twice as strong on a 45° slope as on a 20° slope. And steep slopes often cause skiers to make a harder edge-set to initiate their turns, which disturbs the snowpack considerably. Lastly, an avalanche triggered on a steep slope will flow rapidly and will be less channelled by the terrain: the chance of escape will therefore be greatly reduced.

Most avalanches trigger on slopes steeper than 30°, with slopes of around 40° appearing to be the most dangerous (they are not steep enough to stop snow accumulating, but steep enough to collapse with the least possible additional load). Beware! This does not mean that you are not in danger on shallow-angled slopes. Releases may sometimes occur on such terrain, and avalanches often run out onto flat ground (see pp. 17 and 76).

In case of a route with steep slopes
Avalanche probability: greatly increased
Potential damage: increased

Travelling at the bottom of slopes steeper than 30° or under unsupported slopes steeper than 30°.

Route with Steep Slopes Above

Just as sloping terrain is required for an avalanche release, the same is necessary for its continued flow: the kinetic energy picked up during its motion enables it to cross flat areas and sometimes even to travel uphill for several hundred metres! So it is possible to be in danger even when walking along the flat.

By walking below a steep slope it is possible to break the downslope anchors of the snowpack, thereby triggering an avalanche. It is also possible to trigger avalanches at a distance.

On some days when thaw prevails, it can happen that several avalanches release spontaneously several tens of minutes apart, on several different slopes on the same mountainside.

If the route follows the foot of these slopes (which is typical of valley-bottom roads), you can find yourself in a very tricky situation.

Note: in the mountains, perception of relief can be misleading and you can find yourself at the bottom of a steep slope without noticing. If you are unfamiliar with the terrain, it is useful to consider a 1:25,000 scale map in order to choose the safest route.

In case of a route with steep slopes above
Avalanche probability: increased
Potential damage: increased

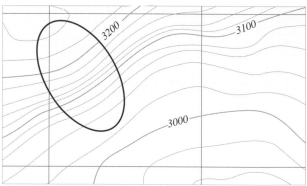

🔍 A slope getting steeper as you descend. Not possible to see the foot of the slope from the top. On the map: contours getting closer together.

Steep
Convex Slopes

On a convex slope, the creep of the snowpack is faster at the bottom than at the top. This results in the creation of tension in the snowpack at breaks of slope. But snow is weak in traction. So breaks of slope tend to promote avalanche release.

Even if there are particularly noticeable breaks in the slope, convexity is a source of instability in the snowpack. So large dome-shaped hills where the slope only steepens very gradually can hold nasty surprises: fractures of the snowpack may happen where the slope is very shallow, and sometimes people are carried down while crossing terrain that is almost flat!

It is therefore better to avoid these dubious areas, which can easily be identified on the map or on the ground.

In case of convex slopes
Avalanche probability: increased
Potential damage: +/- unchanged

Group Member with Poor Technical Skills

In the mountains, it is essential to choose the right route. But it is also essential to be able to follow it!

When in action, an unskilled skier looks mainly at his skis and not at his surroundings. He will instinctively choose the easiest ground... even if it is the most dangerous! Moreover, the novice is also likely to fall, which severely disturbs the snowpack and may cause it to fail. In case of avalanche his chances of escape are minimal (they are already low for an expert skier!). Lastly, it would be difficult for him to carry out a rescue or organise the evacuation of an injured person in difficult terrain. Therefore poor technical skills are a risk factor.

It is not always easy to judge whether one's own technical standard is adequate to undertake a given route safely, the more so because gradings of routes in guidebooks are only general indications – and because the difficulty may vary considerably according to conditions at the time.

   In case of doubt, it is advisable to plan at least one escape route of lesser difficulty.

In case of a group member with poor technical skills
Avalanche probability: increased
Potential damage: increased

Unfit
Group Member

Lack of fitness causes slow progress, but simply being late can be catastrophic. This is especially the case in springtime, when the instability of the snowpack increases as the day goes on: so a group which is too slow can find itself in a very precarious position in a place where, two hours earlier, they would have passed without a problem. So an unfit group which undertakes a long route on a southerly aspect on a fine spring day is undeniably showing a degree of imprudence.

In addition, in case of accident, when it is a race against the clock to save the victims, unfitness may slow down the rescue attempts and have dire consequences.

A group in poor physical condition is therefore more vulnerable and consequently runs greater risks. Also, it is always preferable to stay within one's physical limits and to plan (and not hesitate to take) at least one shorter and less demanding alternative route.

In case of an unfit group member
Avalanche probability: increased
Potential damage: increased

Group Member not Equipped with Shovel, Probe and Transceiver

In considering the rescue of avalanche victims, it is essential to remember that speed is fundamental. The survival chances of someone buried in snow diminish very rapidly with time. Also, a rescue by the members of the group involved in the incident has the best chance of success. Consequently, the most useful rescue equipment is that which can be deployed immediately by the group itself. Transceiver, shovel and probe must be regarded as an indivisible unity. If one group member does not have them, he will be more difficult to recover if buried; and if he is unharmed, he will not be able to find or to dig out anyone else. Thus, the accident very rapidly turns to tragedy.

It should not be thought, however, that transceiver, shovel and probe give protection against all risks. This equipment is only useful if it is in perfect condition, if its use has been mastered (regular training is necessary) and, above all, if it does not encourage liberties to be taken with avalanches.

In case of a group member not equipped with shovel, probe and transceiver
Avalanche probability: +/- unchanged
Potential damage: increased

Party Consisting of More than Five Members or Fewer than Three Members

The safety of a party is firstly dependent on its size. Very large or very small parties are, for different reasons, more vulnerable. If the party is composed of a large number of people, the additional load upon the snowpack will be greater and the area disturbed by the party making a ski descent will be greater, as each person wants to make their own track. So the probability of causing a fracture in the snow layers will be greater. In addition, if the party is large and has to proceed by regrouping in each protected spot, it will be greatly slowed down. But, since conditions may change rapidly, simply being late can have serious consequences, particularly if heavy snowfall or rainfall are taking place. Secondly, if the party is on a route without shelter, there is potential for numerous victims...

On the other hand, if the group consists of less than three members, it will be difficult for them, in case of accident, to carry out a rescue without outside assistance, which reduces the survival chances of possible victims.

In case of a group with more than five members
Avalanche probability: increased
Potential damage: increased

In case of a group with fewer than three members
Avalanche probability: +/- unchanged
Potential damage: increased

Party Without Rescue Training

You have to be well trained (and rather lucky) to find quickly someone carried down by an avalanche. And when victims are found alive, it is not guaranteed that they will stay that way; if not dug out very quickly, they will often be suffering from asphyxia, unconsciousness or cardiac arrest. They may also be suffering from hypothermia and serious injuries (fractures, bleeding, etc.). So, unfortunately, some people die after having been dug out.

Sometimes the survival of an injured person depends on the effectiveness of the first aid he receives. In other words, his fate is in the hands of those who have escaped the avalanche, while they await medical help and evacuation to hospital: if the injured person is badly hurt and if his companions know nothing about rescue, then his chances are slim. The same applies if the evacuation has to be undertaken by a party that has not practised this kind of exercise. So the risk is higher for a party untrained in rescue methods, which of course does not mean that one will be safe if the reverse is true (the outcome of the accident does not always depend on the rescuers!).

In case of a party without rescue training
Avalanche probability: +/- unchanged
Potential damage: increased

ASSESSING RISK

As the problem of estimating avalanche risk is complex, it is as well to approach it methodically.

Risk assessment involves two successive phases: the gathering, then the analysis of information.

Information gathering makes it conveniently possible to determine the weather and snowpack situation, the features of the route taken and the abilities of the party. As the instability of the snowpack at a given moment is largely a function of past meteorological events (and not always very recent ones!), information gathering must span several days. That does not mean that you need to adopt an overly rigorous approach: it is enough to memorise what the weather has been like, consult whatever reports are available and, if there are none, to ask the local information services, mainly ski patrols and tourist offices. For this purpose, use the media of your choice: TV, (Teletext, local channels), newspapers, telephone, Internet, etc.

As regards terrain, maps, guidebooks and topos may be used.

Finally, it is sometimes useful to complete the process by obtaining short- and medium-term weather forecasts (in case of being out for several days). And there is no such thing as too much information.

✔ *Don't economise on information gathering, otherwise your analysis will be founded on sand.*

Local information

D–5	Regional and local information	– Press
D–4		– Telephone information services
D–3		– Internet
D–2		– Radio
D–1		– TV (national, regional and local)
		– 1:50,000 and 1:25,000 maps
		– Guidebooks and topos
D-Day	Local Information	– Telephone information services
Before leaving		– 1:25,000 maps
		– Topos
		– Posted bulletins
		– Ski patrollers
		– Guides
		– Hut wardens
		– Personal observation
On the route	On-site sampling	– Personal observation
		– Information from other parties

Information gathering: Why? What? How?

Information analysis takes place just before leaving. The method of analysis described here is a very simple in-field method: the risk is assessed according to an aggregation of local risk factors (meteorological and snowpack factors, terrain factors and human factors as previously discussed). According to this system, the more numerous the counter-indicating factors are, the more hazardous the situation is estimated to be. Despite the simplicity of this method, it has numerous advantages.

• It serves to pick up on alarm signals which would go unnoticed if you were not looking for them.

• You don't need to worry about any 'threshold' effect: a small variation in conditions cannot lead to a big difference in the result. So it can cope with small imprecisions in observation, because a potential error cannot change the result in a fundamental way.

• It can be used to compare usefully the risk on several different routes in order to determine the safest one.

These advantages are more marked when all the factors used are relevant, numerous, statistically independent and equally weighted. *NivoTest** puts this method into practice by implementing these conditions. So it helps to quickly and logically establish a risk assessment for a given route.

---

a Meteorisk development, see page 108.

Reducing the Risk

It has already been seen that risk is determined by, on the one hand, the probability of avalanche release and, on the other, by potential damage (see Definition of risk, p.30). To limit risk, therefore, both of these need to be reduced as much as possible.

REDUCING THE POSSIBILITY OF AVALANCHE RELEASE

You can considerably reduce the risk of being carried down if the answers to the three following questions are in the affirmative:
• is it reasonable to go out?
• is the route practicable?
• is the slope safe?

Your risk is also reduced if you systematically keep to the safety rules which apply to movement on mountainous terrain (which are described in the following pages). Going into the mountains without considering these questions is a gamble with your own life. To get the most accurate answer you should take into consideration avalanche bulletins, *NivoTest*, maps (1:25,000), guidebooks, local reports, eyewitness information and your own personal observations.

Going out should be avoided *if*		• avalanche hazard* >3 with an inexperienced party
	OR	• avalanche hazard >4
	OR	• extreme weather (present or forecast)
	OR	• party member tired, ill or hurt
	OR	• defective or missing equipment (particularly transceiver, shovel, probe)
The route should be avoided *if*		• *NivoTest* shows = :(
	OR	• local warning (closed area, warning signs)
	OR	• local professionals (ski patrols, guides) advise against
	OR	• serious lateness on the route
The slope should be avoided *if*		• suspect signs (deep accumulations, cracks, etc.)
	OR	• alarm signals ('whumpfing', subsidence, nearby releases)

* Hazard level indicated in the avalanche report

Diagram of the 'Stop or Go' decision

If you arrive at the conclusion that the slope is safe, you should still observe some safety rules (to err is human, especially in avalanche forecasting).

These rules are:
• leave a suitable distance between party members in order to avoid too high additional loads (coming down, go one at a time)

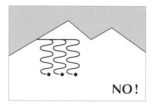

NO!

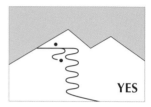

YES

• avoid sudden impacts (jumping cornices, heavy edge sets, falls)
• avoid traversing halfway up or down the slope
• be ready to avoid suspect areas (breaks of slope, areas of high accumulation)
• don't regroup in unstable areas (steep open slopes, convex terrain, slopes below cols).

REDUCING POTENTIAL DAMAGE

Reducing potential damage means: 'Giving yourself more chance of survival in case of avalanche'.* To achieve this, you have to be able to:
• reduce the possibility of being buried
• be easy to find if buried
• survive burial
• get help quickly
• be able to search for a victim effectively
• give first aid
• evacuate a victim.

---

* It is also essential to avoid all behaviour which might cause danger to others.

It is worth noting that the potential damage which threatens a skier depends very much on his companions. So you would be advised not to go out alone, but with company. The various methods aimed at reducing potential damage should never be ignored, as they are to the mountaineer what the life-belt is to the sailor (and no more!).

Reducing the Possibility of Being Buried
You can never be certain of not being buried, even in a small sluff. However, some precautions are worth taking:
- leave enough distance between party members, to reduce the number of people carried down if there is an avalanche (and to maximise the number of people available for searching)
- only regroup in sheltered areas
- avoid narrow gullies and gorges, where snow can accumulate in large quantities
- avoid the use of safety straps and leashes
- look for escape routes with shelter (best to escape to the side)
- be on the lookout for the least sign of release (cracks, noises, subsidence) to be able to warn, stop or run
- and if you are carried down, try to stay on the surface of the avalanche (as you would in a big river).

Being Easy to Find if Buried *(Co-author F. Sivardière)*
Various devices have been invented to enable rescuers to find a
person buried under the snow, amongst them electronic trans-
mitters-receivers sometimes known by the acronym ARVA*
(appareil de recherche de victime en avalanche – device for
finding avalanche victims)– here referred to as a transeiver.

A transceiver in receive mode is able to register and find the
signal sent by a transceiver in send mode. So a person buried by
an avalanche has more chance of being found quickly by his
companions if he is wearing an transceiver in send mode. The
autonomy which this gives parties in terms of rescue means that
their use is strongly recommended.

Transceivers are light (200 to 300g) and small (no bigger than
a Walkman). For several years now, there has been a common
frequency in Europe and North America (457kHz): they are thus
all compatible, irrespective of manufacturer.

*Some of the transceivers on the market today (main types available):
ARVA 9000, Barryvox, Fitre, Ortovox, Pieps, Tracker. They are sold in ski
and mountain equipment shops (price around the same as a good snowboard or pair of skis).*

* or sometimes DVA (detecteur de victime d'avalanche – avalanche victim
detector)

The most recent studies on the chances of survival of buried avalanche victims indicate two fundamental principles as regards their rescue:

- help must come immediately after the accident, for the survival chances of a buried victim diminish very quickly
- immediate rescue organised by those who have escaped the avalanche gives the best chance of success, as it can be immediate.

Transceivers enable the group to start rescue operations right away. They are light, not bulky (which means you can wear them without them getting in the way), reliable and easy to use (if you practise with them), and they both enable you to be found beneath the snow, and you to find a companion. So the transceiver is at present an unavoidable element of the personal equipment for the snow sport devotee in the mountains. However it is not the only element. The shovel and probe are the indispensable complements of the transceiver. The shovel enables the snow to be shifted quickly in order to retrieve the victim. It is incomparably more effective than hands, skis or even snowboards. As for the probe, it can be used to assess the depth of burial, which is important in knowing what pattern of digging to use. But it also proves essential in the phase of the final location of the victim, where it is often quicker than using the transceiver.

While the transceiver should be carried directly on the body every time you go out, switched on and in 'transmit' mode, the shovel and probe equally have their place in the rucksack.

The transceiver is worn under the jacket and switched to 'transmit' mode before leaving base. In the rucksack: shovel and probe, the essential companions.

A transceiver is an electronic device and thus relatively fragile (no impacts, no leaving in the cold or at the bottom of a damp rucksack). Out of season, it should be hung up without batteries in a dry place where it is not exposed to high temperatures. In the summer, the opportunity may be taken to have it serviced by the manufacturer. The batteries are an important element in the proper functioning of transceivers and their condition influences their range (the distance at which a transceiver in 'receive' mode picks up the signal of a transceiver in 'transmit' mode). Use alkaline batteries (not lithium nor rechargeable batteries, which can run down very suddenly). They must be tested regularly and replaced when necessary. As a rule, replacement batteries should give more than 200 hours on transmit, followed by about an hour on receive.

The evening before and on every day out, the correct functioning of the transceiver must be tested, on transmit and receive. It is also recommended to check the range regularly. The range of transceivers is variable: it depends especially on the respective positions of each unit. The range is at its maximum when the aerials of the transceivers are parallel to each other, and at a minimum when they are at right angles. It is essential to ensure a worst case scenario of 15 to 20 metres range.

Checking that the transceiver is working correctly. Unit B must be able to pick up the signal of Unit A and vice versa.

Surviving Burial

The avalanche victim is first of all threatened by asphyxia. So in order to increase your chances of survival during an enforced stay under snow, try to protect the respiratory tracts by keeping a hand over your mouth and nose, especially in an airborne powder avalanche. If buried, it is important to stay calm. And being warmly dressed helps to prevent the struggle against hypothermia.

With a lot of luck, all of this may be useful in case of accident.

Get Help Quickly

When an avalanche happens, it is too late to look at the telephone directory! So emergency numbers must be memorised or held in your mobile phone, or written on a card kept in your jacket.

HELLO, DIRECTORY ENQUIRIES?

✓ *Don't forget to check emergency numbers regularly. General SOS number in Europe is 112.*

Quick alert, quick rescue

The information to give to the rescue service is as follows:

Witness
- Surname, first name
- Place, map reference
- Telephone number
- Radio channel, call sign

Victims
- Number
- Nature of injuries
- Do they have transceivers or other means of location?

Avalanche
- Time of release
- Place (name, map references, altitude)
- Dimensions, other features

Weather
- Visibility
- Precipitation (rain, snow, hail, etc.)
- Wind (speed and direction)

Terrain
- Possibility for landing/winching
- Dangers (obstacles, cables, electricity lines, etc.)

If no radio or phone is available to call for help, you must always carry out a search before sending for help

Searching for a Victim Effectively
With the passing minutes, the victim's chances of survival diminish rapidly. Acting methodically can save precious time. There are certain general principles to follow, whatever search methods you are using.

Unless it endangers you, get onto the avalanche debris and start to search immediately with all available resources below the point where the victim disappeared. If necessary, post a lookout who can give warning in case of new danger – don't forget the rescuers' safety.

Position of the victim at moment of release

Point last seen

Area of first search

Area of first search for avalanche victims

- Begin searching in a downhill direction if coming from above (and vice versa).
- If you find gear belonging to the victim, leave it in place and visible, or mark the spot.
- If there is no result in the area of first search, extend the search sideways.
- If a victim is found, clear snow from his airway and body as quickly as possible (but leave him in the hole), and give first aid and protection.
- Don't dirty the site (food, cigarette ends, etc.) so as not to confuse the work of any rescue dogs.

Searching for victims can go on simultaneously using different methods:

Visual and Auditory Search

Go over the avalanche debris looking for clues (parts of the body sticking out, rucksacks, clothes, skis, etc.) and listening carefully: sometimes calls can be heard if the victim is partly or not deeply buried. Rock, trees and depressions may hold the victim: probe these areas, without delaying there too long.

Searching with Transceivers

- Switch all transceivers to search mode. Anyone not searching must also switch to search mode or switch off so as not to affect the search.
- Take the transceiver in your hand so as to begin searching according to the manufacturer's instructions.
- Search the avalanche debris as quickly as possible, turning the unit in all directions until a signal is received from a transceiver worn by one of the victims. The searching has to be done in a systematic and thorough fashion in order to work quickly and be sure of not leaving any area unexamined.
- When a signal is picked up, find the transmitter. For this there are two techniques, corresponding to the different types of unit: grid searching and induction-line searching. The two methods employ the same principle: the nearer you approach the transmitting unit (and therefore the victim), the stronger the audible signal is.
- For the final phase, use the probe.

✓ *Remember: only regular practice enables efficient use to be made of the transceiver.*

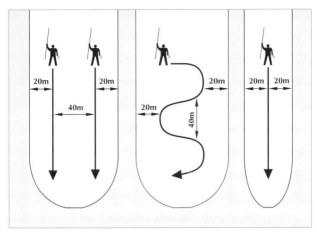

Search patterns with a transceiver (maximum distances shown)

Searching for a victim with transceiver, shovel and probe

Grid Searching

Note: if using this method, do not change the orientation of the unit during the search (or alternatively, keep it vertical).

Begin the search at the point where the victim disappeared. When the first signal is received (C) carry straight on. The signal will grow in strength to a maximum (D) then begin to get weaker (E). Stop when the signal gets weaker (without carrying on to the point where it disappears, to save time) and come back, while turning the signal tuner down one notch. Come back to where the signal was strongest (D). From this point, carry on at right angles to the previous direction (it doesn't matter which side). If the signal gets weaker, stop (F) and come back. Go to the spot where the signal was strongest (D). Carry straight on, keeping to the same method: from D, do the same thing as from C, always turning down the signal tuner (you can mark these points if that helps without losing time).

When you can hear the signal when the tuner is on minimum, the victim is very close (G). Deploy the unit along the snow surface. When the maximum signal is found, quickly find another maximum point (within a one- to two-metre radius) by cross-searching centred on the first maximum point. If a second point is found, the victim will be between the two points; otherwise he will be directly below the first point.

Then probe an area of one to two square metres around this point to locate the victim precisely before digging.

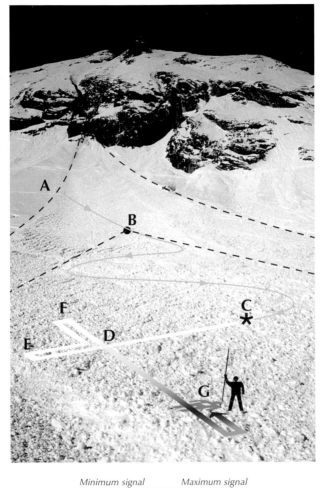

Minimum signal   *Maximum signal*

Conducting a grid search

Induction Line Searching

The principle of this method consists in following the electro-magnetic field lines generated by the victim's transceiver in order to locate him.

When the signal is received (C), turn the transceiver in the horizontal plane to determine the direction to follow. Then walk for several metres in this direction and stop (D) to correct, if necessary, the direction which the transceiver indicates. Repeat the process from point to point (E, F, G, H, I) until the victim's position is reached, whilst appreciating that the path followed will be curved.

Then fix the position of the victim by a grid search on the snow surface, then do the fine location with the probe before digging.

Note: units which are suitable for induction line searching vary from each other, each one have specific technical characteristics. So it is important (before having an accident) to study the maker's instructions for use in order to modify and perfect the general method described above.

Probe Searching

If the victim has no transceiver (which should never happen) or if there are plenty of rescuers and if the area of first search is not too big, it is possible to utilise emergency probing with probes or, if these are not available, skis or ski-sticks.

To carry out this type of probing, the following procedures should be observed:

- line up shoulder to shoulder to form the probe line
- nominate a probe leader who will give the commands to probe and to advance (it is possible for the person to be in the probe line)
- limit the search to the area of first search
- probe once per square metre (one probe every two paces), the probe depth being around one metre*
- wear gloves to prevent a sleeve of ice from forming on the probe
- mark the areas probed if possible and if necessary.

*These suggested values are for an emergency probe, and may need to be changed according to terrain and the characteristics of the debris.

Minimum signal   Maximum signal

Conducting an induction line search

This technique is very slow, especially on steep or broken ground, and gives very little chance of finding victims alive. So its use requires all the more determination and method.

Line probes, which require a large number of people, are generally only used by rescue teams. So it is useful to offer your services to the rescue controller, who will be responsible for organising and directing the teams of searchers.

Line probing

Grid for emergency probing with a small number of rescuers

Giving First Aid *(co-author D. Michellod)*
Some victims die even before the avalanche has come to a halt because of severe trauma which they may have sustained (collision with or crushing due to rocks, trees or blocks of hard snow). But the majority of those carried down die of asphyxia or hypothermia. Most of them are, therefore, alive when the avalanche stops and have a good chance of remaining so if they are found and receive first aid quickly. So immediate aid given by the survivors or witnesses is paramount.

When the victim has been dug out, some simple procedures can be lifesaving.
- Deal first of all with unconscious victims.
- Never leave an injured patient unsupervised.
- Protect the victim against cold (shelter from bad weather and insulate with a jacket, survival blanket, etc.).
- Don't move the victim unnecessarily and without planning.
- If possible, do not evacuate the victim yourself but wait for organised rescue.
- Leave him, dug out of the snow, but in 'his' hole (which will shelter him) until the moment comes for evacuation.
- Talk to and reassure the victim continuously.

Observations	What to do
The patient is unconscious (but breathing)	Stimulate the patient (by talking to him, pinching, etc.) Put the patient in the recovery position with the usual precautions*
The patient is not breathing	Clear the airway* Start artificial respiration*
The patient has no pulse	Start heart massage* and artificial respiration*
The patient is bleeding severely	Elevate the affected limb Apply pressure*

*According to techniques taught on first aid course

First aid applied to an avalanche victim

And if the victim has not been recovered after a quarter of an hour, do not give up! Some lucky people have survived burials of several hours.

Evacuating a Victim (co-author D. Michellod)

Helicopters are very often used, as long as weather permits, for evacuating casualties. For them, it sometimes represent the last chance for survival; but for those participating in the rescue the helicopter can represent a danger. So it is useful for the mountaineer or skier to know how to prepare a landing site, guide the helicopter in and get aboard safely.

Amongst the machines most commonly used for rescue in Europe are the Alouette III, the Écureuil AS 350, the Lama and

Alouette III

the Agusta A109. In the UK the Westland Sea King Mark 3 and 3a are used by the RAF; and the Sea King Mark 5 is used by RN Search and Rescue units. In North America a variety of machines are employed, including the Huey Cobra. Larger helicopters such as the Bell 412 and occasionally the Chinook are also used. In Russia and parts of the Himalaya the Mi-8 is used extensively. Although helicopters are very manoeuvrable, relatively small machines they cannot land just anywhere. Consequently, the landing site should be chosen with care.

Selecting and Preparing the Landing Site

Ideally:
- the landing area should consist of a flat area of 6m x 6m and an area of around 30m x 30m free of all obstacles (trees, pylons, electricity lines, fences, cables, etc.)

- the helicopter should be able to approach and land into the wind, without encountering any obstacle in the landing path or on take-off.

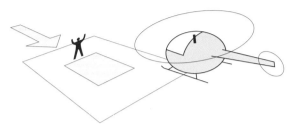

Choice of landing site

Moreover, the landing area must
- be free from areas threatened by other avalanches, by stone fall or ice fall
- be at a distance from the avalanche (so as not to interfere with the search and rescue operations)
- be on a flat area or a rounded knoll, but never in a hollow
- not be on broken ground (rocks, snow pillows) – this is important
- not be in a crevassed area
- be clear of all objects which might blow away as the helicopter levels (clothes, helmets, parapentes, etc.) or which represent obstacles (snowboards, skis and sticks should be laid flat on the ground)
- be pisted (on skis or on foot) if the snow is deep.

Hollow, valley bottom, broken ground: no landing possible!

Guiding the Helicopter In

Landing on the snow surface can be tricky if the pilot lacks reference points to judge accurately the position of his aircraft relative to the ground. When visibility is poor (mist, whiteout, snowfall) or when the snow is powdery and is blown around by the downwash of the rotor, it is helpful to guide the pilot in for landing. This task should be performed by one person, who should:

- establish contact with the pilot if a radio is available
- stand with back to the wind and arms raised in a V shape
- crouch down and stay still when the helicopter is on the point of landing.

Guiding the helicopter in

When the helicopter has landed, stay still and wait for instructions from the pilot or winchman.

Approaching/Embarking

If the rotor is turning, any movements around the helicopter must be made at the invitation of the pilot or winchman, without haste.

It is essential:
- to stay within the pilot's field of vision
- not to approach or go round the helicopter at the back
- to lay snowboards, skis, sticks and probes flat
- if the ground is sloping, not to approach or leave the machine on the uphill side (the ends of the blades can pass very close to the ground!).

If the helicopter cannot land and has to hover in order to make the evacuation, get aboard smoothly and get off without jumping.

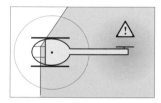

Moving about around a helicopter

✓ *When the rotor is stopping or starting, do not approach the helicopter (risk of blade sailing)!*

Beware! Approaching a helicopter when the rotor is turning requires care. Mistakes can be fatal.

If landing is impossible, the rescuers will winch the victim aboard. Obey their instructions.

Conclusion

In the mountains it is always important to remember that zero risk does not exist and one must always keep off a slope if there is a risk, however small, of endangering someone else.

Otherwise, and as the mountains will always be the fabulous real world that they are, it is up to everyone to make responsible decisions, remembering that giving up a route can sometimes mean that many more can be done elsewhere or later.

For further information

The following organisations offer avalanche training.

Glenmore Lodge National Sports Centre
Aviemore
Inverness-shire
Scotland PH22 1QU
www.glenmorelodge.org.uk

The Mountaineering Council of Scotland
The Old Granary
West Mill Street
Perth
Scotland PH1 5QP
www.mountaineering-scotland.org.uk

Plas y Brenin National Sports Centre
Capel Curig
Conwy
Wales LL24 0ET
www.pyb.org.uk

Training is also offered by individual members of:

The Association of British Mountain Guides and
The Association of Mountaineering Instructors, both at:
Siabod Cottage
Capel Curig
Conwy
Wales LL24 0ET
www.bmg.org.uk
www.ami.org.uk

Canadian Avalanche Association
Box 2759
Revelstoke
BC V0E 2S0
Canada
www.avalanche.ca

Forest Service National Avalanche Center
PO Box 2356
Ketchum
Idaho 83340
USA
www.avalanche.org
Links to avalanche centres in North America

American Institute for Avalanche Research and Education
211 S. Teller
Gunnison
CO 81230
USA
www.avtraining.com
Links to many training providers

New Zealand Mountain Safety Council
PO Box 6027
Wellington
New Zealand
info@mountainsafety.org.nz

METEORISK
CP 993
CH-1951
SION
Switzerland
www.meteorisk.com
tel.: 00 41 (0)79 433 30 72

Using *NivoTest*

NivoTest is a tool for use 'in the field' and assists in estimating avalanche risk on a mountain route as well as in identifying steep slopes (slopes of more than 30°) and taking note of certain safety information. In order to use it properly, it is essential to read the instructions carefully.

NivoTest can be used for:
- estimating the risk for a given route: in this case, it assists in deciding whether to undertake the intended route or not
- comparing the risk for different routes; *NivoTest* can thus help to determine the safest one
- choosing the time, the place or the group according to the accepted risk level.

NivoTest establishes a diagnosis according to the score obtained by the addition of the weights of the risk factors observed in the field. The 'scoring' system has been devised then tested in a large number of real cases. *NivoTest* has been approved by numerous snow professionals (mountain guides, ski patrollers, instructors, experts, engineers and researchers). Nevertheless, it only produces an opinion to compare with other opinions, and must always constitute only one element amongst others in the decision-making process.

Glossary

Aerosol: a suspension of very fine solid or liquid particles

Albedo: the fraction of solar radiation reflected by the snow

Pillow: accumulation of wind-deposited snow

Cornice: accumulation of snow on a ridge or plateau rim, shaped by the wind

Landing area: helicopter landing zone

Temperature gradient: the algebraic difference in temperature between two points, compared to the distance separating them (expressed in °C/m)

Metamorphism: transformations in the snow due to the effect of the energy fluxes within it. These changes particularly affect its crystallography and its cohesion

Graupel: snow characterised by rimed crystals, rounded, often large (around 5mm in diameter); often seen after showers or thunderstorms

Percolation: slow penetration of rain or melt water into the snowpack

Reptation: very slow flow of the snowpack on a slope, varying according to its viscosity

Bergschrund: deep crevasse separating a glacier from the slopes above

Sublimation: direct passage from the solid to the gaseous state

Index

Useful addresses

The telephone numbers of the telephone information services distributing the various avalanche bulletins are numerous … but you can find them all on the Internet. Make sure you note them down at the start of the winter.

Snow and weather information
www.avalanches.org
European avalanche services site, with content in English

www.csac.org
Links to all available on-line avalanche bulletins world-wide

www.metoffice.gov.uk
Links to many national weather services

ISBN-13: 978 185284 473 8

Translation
Blyth Wright

Drawings
Robert Bolognesi: pp. 6, 37, 87, 91, 96, 106

Photographs
Francis Bloch: p15 right
Robert Bolognesi: cover, pp. 4, 7, 8, 9, 10 top, 11,12,13,15 left,
16, 17, 18, 26, 31, 40, 42 top, 42 bottom, 44, 45, 46, 48, 50,
52, 54, 56 middle, 58, 60, 62, 64, 66, 68, 70 top, 72, 74, 76,
83, 88, 89, 90, 91, 97, 99, 100, 102, 111
Vincent Chritin: p10 middle
Bertrand Favre: p10 bottom
Pascal Fournier: p32 top
Pascal Gaspoz: pp. 30 bottom, 32 bottom, 93
Gérald Maret: pp. 25, 30 top, 42 middle
Jean-François Meffre: p29
Jacky Michelet: p23
François Sivardière: pp. 56 top, 56 bottom, 70 bottom
Didier Turc: p14
Robert Volponi: p95

CICERONE

2 POLICE SQUARE, MILNTHORPE, CUMBRIA LA7 7PY
www.cicerone.co.uk